THE
UNSEEN

BY

AYA YATIM RHODES NICKELS

Trilogy Christian Publishers

A Wholly Owned Subsidary of Trinity Broadcasting Network

2442 Michelle Drive

Tustin, CA 92780

Copyright © 2024 by Aya Yatim Rhodes Nickels

All Scripture quotations, unless otherwise noted, taken from the ESV® Bible (The Holy Bible, English Standard Version®), copyright © 2001 by Crossway Bibles, a publishing ministry of Good News Publishers. Used by permission. All rights reserved.

All rights reserved, including the right to reproduce this book or portions thereof in any form whatsoever.

For information, address Trilogy Christian Publishing

Rights Department, 2442 Michelle Drive, Tustin, CA 92780.

Trilogy Christian Publishing/ TBN and colophon are trademarks of Trinity Broadcasting Network.

For information about special discounts for bulk purchases, please contact Trilogy Christian Publishing.

Trilogy Disclaimer: The views and content expressed in this book are those of the author and may not necessarily reflect the views and doctrine of Trilogy Christian Publishing or the Trinity Broadcasting Network.

10 9 8 7 6 5 4 3 2 1

Library of Congress Cataloging-in-Publication Data is available.

ISBN 979-8-89041-718-3

ISBN 979-8-89041-719-0 (ebook)

DEDICATION

To My Jesus

To My Readers

To My Parents

To My Sisters

To My Baba

To My Mama

To My Samwell

To My In-laws

To My Baby Mia

This is our story.

TABLE OF CONTENTS

INTRODUCTION 1

CHAPTER ONE:
FROM THE BEGINNING 4

CHAPTER TWO:
THE LONGEST YEAR 9

CHAPTER THREE:
FOSTER CARE - THE FIGHT 18

CHAPTER FOUR:
MISSED THE LANDING 23

CHAPTER FIVE:
A DREAM CAME TRUE 29

CHAPTER SIX:
THE PURSUIT OF HAPPINESS 41

CHAPTER SEVEN:
THE PERFECT TRAGEDY 51

INTRODUCTION

At a very young age, my grandmother always taught me to never look at the beggars alongside the street and to always maintain a safe distance.

The streets of Beirut, Lebanon could be a very dangerous place for young girls, so it was very important that I kept my distance. As I walked closely alongside my mother, I couldn't help but turn my face to look at them. The entire street was outlined with dismembered mothers with children crying and pleading for mercy. Pleading to *me* for mercy. A 9-year-old girl who had nothing that she could offer them. Despite being 'unseen' by everyone else, I have never forgotten their faces.

I have spent most of my life living in silence, afraid of what the world would think of me if they truly knew my story. Mine is a deep and complicated story about an ordinary girl who had lived an entire lifetime by the age of 28, feeling unseen for most of it. I have spent most of my life relentlessly pondering and searching for the truth. And it wasn't until I finally found my truth that I realized the power it holds to set me free. Only by losing everything, was I able to gain everything.

My wish is that this story of my life would be a lighthouse to anyone who feels lost and confused, seeking peace and joy. Some may find one or the other, but rarely do people find both.

And by grace alone, I found both.

In the most unlikely of places, I learned that pain and suffering doesn't have to end in vain. By surrendering my pain and allowing it to be a part of my healing journey, I finally saw my life transform in ways I never thought were possible.

I hope my story conveys that hope can still be found even in a dark and uncertain world because believing in hope while living in a world filled with so much hate and disappointment is arguably the craziest thing a sane person can do. For some, believing in the tooth fairy is easier than believing in things like love, truth, and hope. It's not the transactional world's love and hope used as currency to gain an advantage over one another. It's not the cheap and seductive lie that if we hope and believe hard enough, anything can come true, because I've learned not everything is true, and not everything should be true. What this world too often claims to offer inevitably costs more than it's worth, with your heart and soul as the payment.

Yet it is in who we are, the person we were created to be,

INTRODUCTION

that we find our truest value. You and I were made for so much more than this world will ever give us permission to be. We were made with a great purpose that transcends anything this world can ever offer. We don't need the world to gain the world, because the world has already been given to us.

CHAPTER ONE:
FROM THE BEGINNING

I hate "get to know you" questions.

Every small engagement in my life seemed to lead to constantly having to overshare the details of my life. It was exhausting. Every part of me tells a deeper story; a story that I didn't necessarily want everyone to know.

Imagine playing a classroom icebreaker and being asked to share a fun fact: "How many siblings do you have?", and this was your answer, "Well, I have two sisters, Tala and Sarah, and one adopted brother, Chris. I also have one biological brother (we don't talk), two half-biological brothers, Amir and Mahumand, and two stepsisters, Katie and JJ, who are twins!"

Like I said, I hate "get to know you" questions. By the time I finish my answer, three people already have questions, so many questions about how, what, when, where and what happened again?

CHAPTER ONE: FROM THE BEGINNING

So here is my actual answer: My mother (Mama) had 6 children, but I am only fully related to 4 of them. I have one older brother and two older half-brothers. We were all about 2 years apart, with me the oldest of the sisters, Tala in the middle, and Sarah as the youngest. My brother is 11 months older than I. And he never let me forget it.

My family lived in the Yatim (our family name) building in the middle of Beirut. My father (Baba) inherited it when his father died. After my father got his pharmaceutical degree and married my mother, they sold the house and opened a family-run pharmacy. Baba lived in that pharmacy.

Since we grew up in a male dominated culture, appearances meant everything. I remember a time when my mother and father got into a screaming match over some weight I had recently gained; I was 4.

We had to stay with my grandparents for a few months while my mother and father were in America giving birth to Sarah. My grandparents were very loving and caring, but only to the people they wanted to be. For them, love was a conditional weapon used to gain power and control. You were only accepted and loved if you met their unrealistic standards of beauty and lifestyle.

Tala did not have this issue. She was the sister everyone loved. She was cute and charming; I was lazy and shy. She was delicate and pure while I was aggressive and chaotic. I spent most of my life hating her because I couldn't be her. No matter how much I tried, I was stuck being me.

When I was living with my grandparents, the only place I felt comfortable was the kitchen. They had a Filipino maid who barely spoke Arabic, yet she was the only person I felt safe to be myself around. She would let me sit with her at night and watch Disney movies and eat pretzel sticks.

One night, my grandmother walked into the kitchen and saw me eating a pretzel stick with her. She instantly walked over and snatched the pretzel out of my hand. She continued to remind me how fat I already was, and how I shouldn't still be hungry after eating dinner. She said that if I didn't lose weight, no one would ever want to marry me; I was 8.

She asked me why I couldn't be like Tala, why I couldn't be sweet and thin like her, why I couldn't be more social and talkative instead of eating all the time. I tried my best, but nothing I did was ever good enough. I always had to be better.

CHAPTER ONE: FROM THE BEGINNING

After returning from America, my parents started to fight a lot. Mama tended to break things when they fought, so we always tried to hide and keep a safe distance.

While my brother and sisters were still sleeping, Mama woke me up one morning and dressed me in a nice dress. Since it was still really early, she just told me to stay quiet and come with her. We got in the car and mama started playing my favorite songs in English. Even though I couldn't really understand the words, I liked the beat.

As we were driving, Mama told me if I chose her, she would take me to see my Auntie Maya (Mama's sister) in England. She told me that if I chose her, she would give me whatever I wanted. She told me if I were to choose her, everything would be okay.

As we entered the building, Baba was waiting for us by the elevator. I never really got to see Baba during the day, he was always working. I would stay up really late to just sit with him while he got ready for bed. Even though he acted excited to see me, I knew something was wrong. He looked sad. He then pulled me in, gave me a big hug and gently whispered, "Aya *habite*, choose Mama." I remember looking up at him and thinking, *But I want you.*

The doors opened and a tall woman approached me and took me into an office with a government official sitting behind a huge desk. After what seemed like an eternity of just watching him write, he looked up and asked me one question: "Who do you want?"

God only knows how much I wanted to say Baba. I've always wanted Baba; Mama was too manic and unpredictable. But he told me to choose her, so I did. That was how I found out they were getting a divorce and how Mama ended up with full custody.

Little did I know that my answer to that one simple question would define our entire lives.

CHAPTER TWO: THE LONGEST YEAR

I remember the day we left Lebanon as if it were yesterday. I was 9 years old when my mother randomly woke us all up and told us to start packing. In the corner of my eye, I caught a glimpse of Baba shaking his head on the phone.

It wasn't until we were sitting at the airport waiting to board the plane when she finally told us we were going to England. Mama never liked to tell us her plans. She liked to keep those to herself. I asked her about Baba, and she just looked at me and said, "He's staying back to take care of the pharmacy." He was always at the pharmacy.

When we arrived in Manchester, England, Auntie Maya picked us up from the airport and took us to a nearby motel. I loved my aunt. She was the mom I begged to have. She was everything I wanted to be or could hope to be. Like the rest of my family, she was a Sunni Muslim; therefore, she always had to wear her head covered. But she wore the most stylish clothes, and always put her whole heart into everything she did. The devotion she has to her faith is something I will always admire.

I hated living with my mother. Chaos seemed to follow her everywhere she went. Her mental state had been fragile for a long time. Since Mama grew up during the Lebanese Civil War, she struggled to recover and was never able to gain stability. She first started exhibiting symptoms when she was 15. Her delusions back then weren't as severe. However, as she got older, her hallucinations grew darker. She started to become very paranoid and eventually developed schizophrenia. She believed that the Lebanese government was after her. Everything seemed to trigger her, so she desperately wanted out of Lebanon. She wanted to seek a refuge away from her fears (aka the Lebanese government).

Back then I didn't understand the driving forces that led her fears, but what I did know was that they controlled our entire lives. When we arrived at the motel, it seemed nice. Our room only had two twin beds for the five of us, so it got a little cramped. We ended up staying at that motel for 5 months. In that same span of 5 months, my whole life changed. Everything seemed backwards, and I didn't know how to think or breathe anymore. The best I could describe it is survival mode–do what

CHAPTER TWO: THE LONGEST YEAR

you need to do to get through the day.

Since Baba was born in a British colony, he was able to obtain dual citizenship in Lebanon and England. This made us eligible for British citizenship as well. However, for us to obtain our citizenship, we all needed to live in England for at least one year. The plan was for us to live in England for a year, get our citizenship, and then apply for permanent residency. During those months, my aunt helped Mama enroll us in school for the first time. Baba attempted to put us in kindergarten in Lebanon, but Mama kept pulling us out of school to keep us with her, so we just ended up staying home. Lebanon doesn't have any educational laws or mandates that require parents to send their children to school. As an underdeveloped, war-torn country, education was seen as a privilege, not a right or a basic human need.

Since none of my sisters nor my brother had had any prior schooling, the British school system opted to place us in grades appropriate for our age. My brother and I were placed in the 6th grade, Tala in 4th, and Sarah in 3rd.

Meanwhile, the situation with Mama's mental health seemed to only get worse. My aunt did everything she could to help, but there was only so much a person could do. We all knew she was getting worse, but no one knew how to help. But when Mama called an ambulance to pick her up because "someone was hypnotizing her in her sleep," I knew we had hit rock bottom.

At the end of our 10th month, my sisters and I came home one day to Mama telling us to start packing. Again. Except this time, it was 'just' for the weekend away in Washington DC.

I, now a naïve 12-year-old, was blindly excited for the "weekend" getaway, not because I wanted to go to America, but because I had an English paper due Monday, and leaving the country would be a good excuse for not turning it in on time. My poor 6th-grade English teacher never got that paper.

Once we arrived in Washington D.C., it didn't take Mama too long before she managed to get a car and an apartment. I remember her bursting into our motel room, saying how she got us a house. It was not a house. It was a 2-bedroom apartment in the middle of the Arlington projects. She thought the neighborhood looked nice. It wasn't the apartment I hoped for, but I was convinced I could make it work. At this point I'd learned one thing about life. When giving up isn't an option, the only thing left is to get through it. So my brother took one

CHAPTER TWO: THE LONGEST YEAR

bedroom, and my sisters and I took the other. Mama mostly slept on the couch in the living room. We didn't have a washing machine, so there were dirty clothes everywhere--and I mean everywhere. We rarely had food in the apartment. I remember one day coming home from school and trying to make myself a Nutella sandwich. When I found the jar, I saw it was covered in ants inside and out. Mama was prone to disappear for days, sometimes weeks, without a notice, so my brother and I took on the responsibilities of caring for Tala and Sarah.

Eventually, we all got enrolled in school again. My brother and I were enrolled in 7th grade at Williamsburg Middle School, while my sisters went to Glebe Elementary. To be honest, I loved going to school. It was the only place where I didn't have to care for or rescue anyone. It was my safe place, and I will never forget my math teacher Ms. McDarment. Despite my obvious knowledge gap and underdeveloped skills, she never made me feel stupid or incapable. I used to enjoy going to her after-school help class, mainly because she would bring banana bread. But when my brother found out, he told me I couldn't go anymore.

He really didn't like us leaving the house. One day, Tala and Sarah asked me if I could take them to the park. I knew they missed playing outside, but I didn't want to risk my brother finding out. When I saw the sad and defeated look on their faces, I thought maybe if we just went for a few minutes, he wouldn't find out.

When we got to the park, Tala and Sarah ran to the swings with so much freedom and joy. I had not seen them laugh so much since we left Lebanon. But for at least those 10 minutes, their world was okay, and that made me feel okay.

On our way back, I realized that we probably stayed a little longer than we should have. As we got back into the house, I saw my brother sitting and waiting for us with a couple of his friends. I told Tala and Sarah to go to our room, close the door, and watch T.V. After they were gone, my brother walked up really close to my face and asked me where I had taken them. I told him I just took them to the park for a few minutes and that I didn't think it would take that long. But before I could say I was sorry, my brother grabbed my neck and slammed me against the wall. Holding me there, he looked right at me and asked who I thought I was to disobey him.

After a few minutes of struggling, his friends tore him off

CHAPTER TWO: THE LONGEST YEAR

me, yelling that I wasn't breathing. He let go of my neck, shoved me to the ground, and told me never to do something like that again.

A few nights later, my brother woke me with a disturbed look on his face. I was shocked at first because I had never seen him look so troubled. He pulled me away from Tala and Sarah and told me he saw Mama having sex with a random guy in his bedroom. He just stood there frozen, completely unable to process what he had just witnessed. I was mainly just confused. No one had really explained to me what sex really was, but apparently, it wasn't something that could be good since my brother seemed so disturbed from seeing it.

A week later, he started experimenting with it for himself-- on me.

I felt like a prisoner--a prisoner of my own mind stuck on an endless loop of flashbacks. Each second of those memories causes my whole body to shake. I kept replaying the image of Tala and Sarah playing in the corner with a big toy chest, my brother walking into the room and telling me he wanted to play. He never wanted to play with me, so I thought he was trying to be nice.

We were playing "wrestling" when he pinned me to the floor about 5 feet away from Tala and Sarah. Making sure my sisters were still preoccupied with playing, my brother started to unbutton my pants.

At first, I didn't really realize what was going on, I thought he was still playing, and when I started to feel really scared and exposed, I tried to tell him to get off, but he just kept going, demanding I stay quiet. I tried to scream, but he just covered my mouth so Tala and Sarah couldn't hear me.

After a while, I stopped feeling anything. It was like my whole being turned inward and stayed there. Everything just felt really cold. My heart felt really cold. It felt like something was taken from me. Something special in me that was only meant to be given away freely, not taken by force and manipulation.

We ended up living in that apartment for a year before getting evicted. It was around that time that social services began to show up. They first started by doing random home visits and then talking to my guidance counselor at school. There had been reports made concerning our lack of hygiene and major bruising on my body. It wasn't until I caught a bad stomach flu with a 105.4° fever that someone finally had to step in.

CHAPTER TWO: THE LONGEST YEAR

Thankfully we had a neighbor who came to check in on me. After a week of unsuccessful attempts to convince Mama to take me to the hospital, our neighbor ended up having to kidnap me and take me to the emergency room.

After a few weeks went by, everything seemed to be back to normal. But I still had this nagging feeling in my chest that I knew something wasn't right. That night, I had one of my worst dreams. In my dream, the police arrived at our door and grabbed Tala and Sarah away. There was a lot of screaming and fighting, with blood everywhere. I woke up drenched in sweat with my heart pounding. I knew it was just a dream, but no amount of reason was going to make that nagging feeling go away.

CHAPTER THREE:
FOSTER CARE - THE FIGHT

I will never forget the day I was taken away.

It started out like any other day, I woke up, got dressed and went to school. I was sitting in my home ec class learning how to sew a pillow sham when the classroom phone rang. Since my chair was near the teacher's desk, I could hear the person say my name on the phone. Even though I'd already heard it, she sent shivers down my back when she called my name out loud to go to the office to be picked up early.

As I was walking down the hallway, I knew it couldn't be my mother picking me up. I hadn't even seen her in a few weeks, and even if she were around, she was never on time for anything. There was no world where she would be picking me up early.

At this point, my life seemed to be held together by such a small thread. My life seemed like a game of Russian roulette. No matter how many times the gun missed me, eventually, I knew I would be shot. It was just a matter of time.

CHAPTER THREE: FOSTER CARE - THE FIGHT

When I arrived at the office, I saw a woman dressed in a suit and heels. The principal looked at me and stated I would be leaving with her. The fact I didn't even know anything about "stranger danger" should say something.

On our way to the DHS (Dept of Human Services) office, I asked the social worker about my brother and sisters, and she just said that my brother was already there, and Tala and Sarah were being picked up right now.

As soon as we got to the DHS office, I saw my brother playing on an office computer. I noticed a phone beside him and realized I hadn't told Mama where I was. So I picked up the phone and dialed her cell. When she picked up the phone, all I could hear was her crying and screaming for me to come back. The cry of a mother losing her children is not something anyone can forget.

The social worker saw me getting upset and quickly hung up the phone. I had no idea what was happening, why we were there, or when we were going back home. The social worker took me into a playroom with my brother and sat us on the couch. She began to tell us why we had been taken away and that we would not be able to go home again. She told us that

Mama had severe paranoid schizophrenia and that it wasn't safe to live with her anymore.

It took me a second to process everything. I had just left my whole life behind, and all I had left were the clothes I was wearing. A black flowy skirt, a T-shirt and boots. Everything else was gone. It may not have been much, but it was all I had left. But now it was all gone. After sitting next to my brother silently for a few minutes, he leaned over to me and whispered, "This is your fault, isn't it?" I instantly pulled away from him and started crying. He was right; this was my fault.

I was the one who got sick and had to go to the emergency room. I was the one who talked to the guidance counselor and told her about the physical abuse. And now I was the one who was responsible for all of us being taken away.

A couple of hours went by, and I still hadn't seen or heard anything from Tala and Sarah. I started to question whether they were even okay. When they finally did arrive, they both ran up to tell me how our mother had fled with them from the police.

Apparently, after realizing that my brother was taken, our

CHAPTER THREE: FOSTER CARE - THE FIGHT

mother went and picked up Tala and Sarah from their school and drove them around D.C. so that Social Services couldn't find them. However, she made the mistake of returning home, because the police were there waiting. They told Tala and Sarah they had five minutes to grab a few things.

Once we were all together, the social worker explained that we all would be placed in an emergency foster home for the night. My brother would be separated from us and would be staying in a separate foster home. DHS needed time to figure out who would be willing to take in 3 pre-teen girls from a different country. As an aside, when all of this was happening, my siblings and I were on a temporary student visa and had only been in the country for 9 months. Our main language was still Arabic, so we didn't know what was happening.

When we first arrived at our emergency foster parents' home, I was shocked by how nice and big their house was. They were very welcoming and polite and tried their hardest to make this situation feel as normal as possible. Nothing about this felt normal. They took my sisters and me to Goodwill the next day and got us a few things. During our time together, they loved to take us to places like ball games, hiking, dinner events, etc. We had all kinds of game nights and movie nights. It started to feel like we were almost a real family.

Even though this was supposed to be a temporary placement, our foster parents let us stay longer while our case manager continued to work with my father to regain custody. The judge wouldn't allow my father to take us back home because Lebanon was considered a combat zone (and still is). The judge would only grant him custody if he moved all of us to England.

Auntie Maya and my mom's younger brother Uncle Karim, who was also in England, were able to help Baba make arrangements for us to be able to return. The night before we left, I was packing and found a small, pink wallet under the bed and fell in love with it. I placed the wallet on top of the dresser to ask my foster mom if I could use it to carry my passport instead of carrying my backpack. In the morning, I was running late (as usual) and decided just to leave it behind.

I was so excited to go back home. I knew Baba would take care of everything.

I could finally breathe for the first time since all of this started.

CHAPTER FOUR:
MISSED THE LANDING

We arrived at the airport right as Baba's plane was supposed to land, so we stood at the gates waiting for him to come out.

My sisters and I just sat there waiting as everyone else walked by, thinking maybe his flight got delayed.

After a few hours, our social worker decided it would be best to take us back to our foster home and figure out why he never showed up.

When we returned to the house, our foster parents sat the three of us down and told us that we would be placed in a different foster home. Shocked, I asked them why. My foster mother pulled out the pink wallet and said they no longer felt comfortable having us in the house.

My whole body froze. She had found the wallet on top of the dresser and thought I had stolen it. I tried to explain and apologize, but she had already decided who I was to her. There was no point in trying to tell her any differently at that point.

That's the funny thing about foster care, everyone you meet has already been "debriefed" on who you are based on the notes they have. You seem to be only seen through somebody else's eyes, and the real you only exists in theory; but whether you are real or not, you are not heard.

The next day, social services placed my younger sisters together in a new home. I was separated and placed in a separate home. A week after my father didn't show, I had not heard anything from my social worker. Being understandably an anxious hot mess, I called her repeatedly until she broke down and told me what was happening. My heart dropped to my knees as my social worker explained that my father wasn't coming.

He wasn't coming? Like, no one was coming?

I was alone. I felt alone. Who knew one phone call could ruin your whole life? Within that five-minute phone call, I went from having a huge family to being an orphan. An orphan who was abandoned.

By then, since I was older, I knew not to hope for a family. It was decided that a group home would be the most appropriate fit

CHAPTER FOUR: MISSED THE LANDING

for me as I aged. In the end, I was in over a dozen foster homes or group homes. My last group home was the most significant. I was placed in that group home with 12 other girls who were all around the same age as me. I had just turned 13 and was the youngest this home would accept.

As the youngest, I looked up to the other girls, and they looked out after me. They taught me so much, from how to brush my teeth to celebrating my first birthday (at 13). I had never known when my birthday was until I entered the system, and it was documented, so the girls decided to throw me a surprise party in our basement classroom.

At this point, I only wanted to be back with my sisters. I knew the only way would happen if we got adopted together. But the odds of that happening were not in my favor.

After a half year of looking, our social worker found a Lebanese family in Virginia who wanted to adopt us. We all got excited about the idea of being back together and being a family again. We were also excited to be with other people with the same cultural background who could understand us.

As we moved forward with the adoption process, the family

realized that taking on all of us, along with Tala's health condition and my older age, was too much for them to handle, so they withdrew the adoption.

As a last-ditch effort, our social worker arranged for us to be featured on Wednesday's Child, a local news program featuring kids in foster care waiting on adoption, as three Lebanese girls looking for a family. We all got dressed up, and for some ungodly reason, I decided to get a haircut the day before (big mistake, ladies).

Once the segment aired, we all, including our social worker, were shocked by the number of families who seemed interested in adopting us. I don't think many people realize that the dream of adopting and the reality of adopting are two very different things. But we did find a family because of that segment, and parents who took us in as their own. Their story is worth telling, and our adoption story began with a phone call over the previous Memorial Day weekend.

It was the day that Baba didn't show up at the airport. Since we were supposed to be with him and couldn't return to our previous foster family, we needed emergency placement again. That was when Amy Rhodes, who became my mom, first

CHAPTER FOUR: MISSED THE LANDING

received a phone call about us.

My mom went into panic mode. Their adoption home study was not completed, so they were not qualified as adoptive parents yet. Not to mention that Grandma Rhodes, Uncle Chuck, Aunt Gayle, and their son, Dan, were staying at the house for the weekend while my new Dad, Dave, was out of the country. She had to say no.

Five months later, my future parents were told by their adoption agency, the Barker Foundation, that Barker felt they had found a match for them. He was a 12-year-old boy and had been featured on Wednesday's Child. My mom was sent the link to the Wednesday's Child clip to look at before meeting with their social worker. The link wouldn't work. My mom may be technology-challenged, but even she knows how to open a link. But no matter what she tried, the link did not want to work.

When my dad got home from a business trip, on a Wednesday, she told him the link wasn't working and that they couldn't go into the meeting with the social worker the next day without even watching the video. So my parents sat down together and once again clicked the link – the same one my mom had clicked, and it had not worked – and immediately, Wednesday's Child popped up. The new Wednesday's Child segment featured the three of us.

My future parents were stunned, and immediately felt God's handiwork. "These seem to be the same three girls we got a call about in May." In fact, all that summer, they had wondered what had happened to us three. Had we been adopted? Were we happy? Where were we? When they saw the segment with us, they knew God was telling them, "I told you these girls are your family; go make it happen!"

So they marched into Barker the next day and told them that while they were sure the young man was wonderful, God had shown them that the three girls would complete their family.

CHAPTER FIVE:
A DREAM CAME TRUE

At the beginning of our adoption, life felt like a fairytale, just like a honeymoon. I was finally reunited with my sisters and a part of a healthy and loving family.

During my time in foster care, I felt completely out of control of everything in my life. I had been to over a dozen foster homes and group homes where everything from the minute I woke up to the second I went to sleep was decided by someone else. Every decision concerning me was already decided and planned, ready to be executed. I was just the person they needed to fill in. But not anymore; I had a new life now.

Everything felt so new and exciting, like the first time I got my own room, which my parents let me decorate to my heart's content (aka a hot pink wall). They gave me my first cellphone, took me to my first baseball game, and even celebrated Christmas for the first time. They attended every musical I was in with flowers. We were all excited to be a complete family. It felt like a dream come true. But every dreamer must wake up one day.

As I was settling into this new life, my past life started to catch up with me. I became even more determined to put everything behind me and fully embrace my new identity. But after the newness and excitement began to wear off, I started to feel extremely conflicted.

On my adoption day, I awoke as Aya Maged Yatim and then went to bed as Aya Yatim Rhodes. Overnight, I had become a new person with a new name, home, and family. All I wanted was to be able to embrace this new life. But no matter how much the outside changed, my heart kept reminding me of one unfortunate truth: I was still the same Aya.

Still the same Aya who didn't understand why her father left her behind. Still the same Aya who spent most of her life living in the Arab world. Living in Islamic tradition and culture, I had no idea what it meant to be an American. I was granted full citizenship into a country I hardly knew.

I had to learn so many new rules - both the rules of my adoptive family and the rules of how to be a teenage girl in high school. Not a simple task. I was expected to know and obey all cultural norms like how to dress and act appropriately at school and holidays and family gatherings.

CHAPTER FIVE: A DREAM CAME TRUE

To say I was way out of my league would have been an understatement. Yet I was still responsible for keeping up with all my peers academically and socially. And if I slipped up at any moment, everyone quickly reminded me. I realize now they were trying to help me, but as a traumatized 14-year-old girl, I always felt attacked.

It felt as if I was suffocating slowly every day. I was too traumatized to understand what was happening and that was paralyzing. I was always scared and always on edge. I was constantly acting out, so everyone saw how bad I was struggling. At one point, my parents felt as if they had to hide away the knives because they didn't feel safe around me anymore. They were never in any real danger, but trauma can be very unpredictable, so it's better to be safe than sorry. But also understand that none of us really knew nor understood why this was happening to me. All we knew was that I was not okay, and that I needed help. But back then, the effects of trauma on child development were not as well studied or accepted. And in more severe cases like mine, it can be difficult to diagnose and treat. But from my perspective, everything felt like a blur. I would behave in ways I didn't recognize and would say the meanest things to my parents. I was hurting, and I couldn't understand why they weren't. Not that my parents were not sympathetic to my past, they just didn't know the weight it carried.

I hated who I was. It wasn't the real me. The real me was buried under years of abuse and neglect, so I never got the chance to develop—well, anything. I didn't know how to be me because there was no me.

That fall, I started my sophomore year of high school. All I wanted was to fit in. I'd been this weird foreign foster kid for so long, and it felt like everyone knew my story before I had a chance to even to tell it. I wanted to take charge of my narrative. I wanted to be my own hero. I thought I was going to become this whole new person. The person I always wanted to be.

Yet instead of trying to change the inside, I thought it would be easier just to change the outside. I tried to get into random hobbies and sports but was not built for that life. I am not athletic and will never be athletic.

No matter how hard I tried, I would never magically become someone else. I was always going to be stuck being me, a weird nobody. I slowly turned inward and shut everyone out. It was

CHAPTER FIVE: A DREAM CAME TRUE

easier that way. At least it was for the time being. Until one day on Christmas Eve, I came home from spending the night with a friend to see everyone busy getting ready to go over to my adoptive grandparent's apartment for a family dinner.

Earlier that day, I discovered that the guy I was "talking" to didn't like me and was just using me, so the last thing I wanted to do was go visit a person I hardly knew at the time. It was not because I didn't want to see him, but because I didn't want him to see me. I did not want to be seen.

As I went upstairs, I heard my dad telling me how late I was and that I needed to hurry up to get ready. At this point, I had known my new grandfather for less than a year, and the fact that I had to stuff my pain again and put on a fake, happy smile was just too much to ask. Though I became an expert at putting on a brave and happy face, even I have my limits.

When my dad walked into my room, I was so upset I pushed him away, telling him to get out of my room. I don't know what happened inside, but something in me just snapped. My dad tried to take hold of my hands to stop me from hitting him, but again, in complete survival mode, I pushed him out of the door. Instead of allowing him to comfort me, I forced him away.

Back then, I didn't have the capacity to see my dad's loving intentions. To me love felt almost like a cruel joke. I had never experienced that kind of love and consideration before, it felt dangerous to me. Because I knew it was something I desperately wanted and needed, but not something I was willing to risk losing again.

So I left and went back to my friend's house. My dad and brother, Chris, followed me back to her house to ensure I was safe and tried to convince me to go back home. But everything felt so raw, and I felt so guilty for the way I treated my dad, I knew I couldn't or even shouldn't go back.

I already felt terrible about ruining my sisters' Christmas Eve, and I didn't want to ruin any more of it. It was supposed to be our first Christmas together, and I spent it shouting and arguing. All those times of dreaming about our first Christmas together and I spent it with my friend's family instead of mine. My heart ached as I watched her open all the gifts with her family the next morning. I wanted that. I wanted her family. I wanted to have parents who loved me enough to not only know what I liked but went out of their way to shower me with it.

The next day, I came home to an empty house. It was a

CHAPTER FIVE: A DREAM CAME TRUE

relief. I went up to my bedroom and opened my door to find my queen-sized bed filled with presents. On top of everything was a box of Coco Puffs, just lying there. My mom knew I loved Coco Puffs? Words cannot describe the amount of guilt and shame that ran through my body at that moment. As I stood there, looking at all the love and care my new parents just gave me, I couldn't take it anymore. I couldn't keep hurting the people in my life who were trying to love me. It wasn't fair to them--or to me. So I knew what I had to do.

It felt like such a simple and painless solution to everyone's problems. With me gone, everything would be okay. I knew what to do. It was easy; all I had to do was take all my prescription medications at once and hope it stopped my heart fast enough to kill me before I felt anything. Simple. Easy. Painless. I knew what I had to do.

As I took the pills and began to swallow, I saw an image in my head of Tala and Sarah coming home to find me there, lying dead on the floor. That image broke me. I couldn't do that to them. They had already been through enough, and I was not going to be another person to add to their suffering. So I took a deep breath, spit out everything, and fell to my knees crying.

My mom and dad tried to get me the help I needed. I went to several different treatment centers, including inpatient and outpatient. I remember the first time my dad had to admit me into the treatment center like it was yesterday.

After another intense argument with my parents, my dad told me to get in the car. It was past 9 p.m., so I didn't know where he was taking me. When we got to the facility's parking lot, I looked up at my dad and said, "No, absolutely not. Just put me back in foster care; anything would be better than this." My dad looked at me with a stern look on his face and said, "Is that what you want?" I said, "No, I don't know what I want; that's the problem!" I looked at my dad, waiting for his response, but he didn't say anything. After a long pause, I started seeing tears running down his face. He said, "Aya, I really don't know what else to do, I'm just trying to help you."

At that moment, I realized what I'd done. My dad was a colonel in the Air Force; he flew fighter jets in Afghanistan. He does not cry, yet here he was crying… for me. I didn't realize the emotional toll I was taking on everyone. It wasn't fair. So I took a deep breath, got out of the car, and said, "Okay, I will try." I was so mad at him; I didn't hug him or say a thing. I just walked away.

CHAPTER FIVE: A DREAM CAME TRUE

The facility looked like an isolated hospital wing, with big, locked doors requiring a badge to open. My mom packed me a duffle bag with enough clothes to last me 4 days. They took me into a private room and searched through all my belongings, documenting each item.

As a 15-year-old, I was mortified that a strange man was not just seeing my underwear but carefully examining each pair to ensure I didn't hide any contraband. They locked up everything, from my cell phone to my bobby pins. After they were done, they escorted me to my room, which consisted of twin beds and nightstands. The mattress was just a thick sleep mat with sterilized sheets and blankets. But at that point, I didn't care what the bed felt like, I just wanted to fall asleep and escape this nightmare, at least until morning.

I had been through this long enough to know the first day was always the hardest. We had different forms of therapy during the day, and then "fun activities" at night. My parents and sisters would come and visit. Seeing my sisters happily living their lives without me made me question if I had made the right choice by getting adopted. Why did I ever think getting adopted at 16 was a good idea? I knew no one could just take a stranger and love them as their own. I knew it was too good to be true.

It wasn't until I graduated high school and returned to England that I finally started my healing journey. My Uncle Karim offered to fly me over to stay with him and my Auntie Maya for a month. I would spend two weeks with him and his family, and then two weeks with Auntie Maya. I was really excited to go. So on my high school graduation day, my parents and sisters took me out for a celebratory lunch after the ceremony and then dropped me off at the airport.

Once I arrived, they asked me if it would be okay if Baba flew over and met me here in London. It had been over 4 years since I had last seen him.

When Baba arrived at the airport, I had no idea what to expect or how to feel. So much had happened between us, so much I didn't fully understand yet. But the minute he stepped out of the gate, and I saw his face, everything felt okay. As if no time had passed between us. Sure, I looked different since he last saw me when I was 11 years old. But he hadn't aged or changed that much. He was still the same Baba to me, and I was still his little girl. He was still the only one that could make me smile and laugh. He was still the only one I would

CHAPTER FIVE: A DREAM CAME TRUE

stay up all night waiting to come home. I ran to him with open arms, embracing him with every part of my being. We ended up spending a whole week together exploring London.

As amazing as our time together was, I knew I couldn't let him leave without asking him to hear his side of the story. It would have bothered me forever. So after a great afternoon of touring castles and gardens, I sat Baba down and asked him what happened. A long series of unfortunate events all boiled down to the pharmacy. He couldn't leave the pharmacy behind. It was his home. He did the best that he could with the options he was given.

Looking at him across from me with so much guilt and shame in his eyes was enough of an apology for me. He was hurting enough for both of us. He knew what he did, and he regrets it to this day. I didn't want to live my life, wishing things could have been different.

After that, my heart felt lighter. After seeing and talking to him, I realized I didn't have to lose him as my father. Though I kept my last name as my middle name, I didn't need it anymore to feel connected to him. I didn't want my past to dictate my future. Somehow, it was okay to live in two different worlds, because our love for one another was still the same.

After I got back home, I felt like a different person. As if there was a storm inside me that finally calmed, and I could breathe again. When my dad picked me up from the airport, he even said that after talking to me for 10 minutes, he knew something had changed. I told him that now that I had some closure, I finally felt ready to start the next chapter of my life.

CHAPTER SIX:
THE PURSUIT OF HAPPINESS

Like most 18-year-olds, college would be my big adventure: college life, college parties, college boys, I was ready.

I was accepted into Radford University, a small-town college next to Virginia Tech. I was the first woman in my family ever to go to college. Most women in my family barely graduated high school, so I wanted to make them proud or, at the very least, graduate.

When I first got to college, I wanted to start a new life and be someone new, again. (How many people can one person be?) This time, I had the opportunity to be a person without a past or a label--a clean slate. I would figure out how to make friends and be a normal young adult. I may have spent most of my high school years going between foster homes and behavioral centers (juvenile loony bins), but not anymore!

I threw myself into the college experience. I joined a sorority, went to parties, made friends, drank the drinks, danced on the tables, and went home feeling worthless and empty every night.

I thought to myself, *Is that it? Is this the great life everyone talks about? A party filled with empty drinks and lost people?* I felt disappointed, almost betrayed. I lost everything and survived every single thing for this?

I remember walking down my college dorm and noticing a flier posted for Cru, a Christian organization on campus. I thought to myself, *Ha! Yeah, right; if I were to go to this, I would give everyone a heart attack. I am way too broken for them. I was looking for something to make me happy, not make me change. I've had enough of that to last me a lifetime.* So I said nope and walked away.

I was born into a Sunni Muslim family in Lebanon. I grew up fasting and bowing down 7 times a day. I grew up listening to the loud ringing of a bell in the middle of the night, alerting everyone that it was time to pray. I grew up learning that Allah is the one and only true god. And though he was a kind and merciful god, you never knew where you stood with him until judgment day. Allah would choose to forgive whom he chose to forgive.

That is why Muslims work so hard to please him, hoping that one day, he will find favor and forgive them. Even my 8-year-

CHAPTER SIX: THE PURSUIT OF HAPPINESS

old mind knew I had no chance of winning his love. I was never going to be good enough. So I silently obeyed, hoping that there was a God out there that would be willing to love me.

It wasn't until I was placed in my first group home that I learned what Christianity was. During my first weekend at home, one of the supervising staff asked me if I wanted to go to church with them. In broken English, I replied "Sure, there's nothing else to do on a Sunday". That seemed to make everyone laugh as if I intended to make a joke. But at this point, I barely knew what a church even was, so I wasn't laughing, just mainly confused. When we got to the church, it was nothing like I had expected. There were chairs everywhere. I sat down at the very end of the row with the rest of my foster sisters. It felt like everywhere we went, everyone knew us as the "foster kids." As I sat there, trying to understand what the pastor was saying, I felt a gush of wind run through me. I remember looking around my seat to find a vent or an open door, but there was nothing. At the very end of the service, the pastor asked if there was anyone who wanted to accept Jesus into their life. I stood up thinking it was a part of the service, and as I was walking down the aisle to meet him, I had no idea what I was doing or even why. All

I knew was it felt right. When we got back to the group home, everyone was congratulating me on converting from Islam to Christianity. I didn't even know that switching religions was even allowed. My foster sister asked me what I wanted to eat for my celebratory lunch. I said, "Pizza. Pepperoni pizza." She laughed then got very serious for a second and asked me "Aya, did you just become a Christian so that you could eat the pepperoni?" I burst out laughing, shaking my head no, but once I was able to speak, I said "Maybe? Yes." Because that was the truth. I didn't want to follow a God who made me swear off pork. I did not want to follow a god who was consistently keeping a record of every fault. I wanted to worship a God who wouldn't care about whether or not I ate a pepperoni pizza and needed to atone for it. So yeah, I became a Christian so that I could eat a pepperoni pizza, and I stand by that decision. It was like a big weight was lifted off my shoulders.

But it wasn't until 3 years later when I was adopted that I actually got to experience and know what church and Christians were truly like. My mom and dad valued their faith and wanted us to experience what it was like to be a part of the church. It was early in our adoption, so my sisters and I agreed without

CHAPTER SIX: THE PURSUIT OF HAPPINESS

question. My parents thought it was important that we had a fresh start as a family and found a nearby Lutheran Church with a great kids' program.

My sisters and I first began by signing up for a ski trip with the rest of the kids at church. There was a newly hired 22-year-old youth pastor, we will call him David, and like any normal 15-year-old, I instantly developed a huge crush on him. In efforts to win him over, I took interest in learning more about the Bible. However, everything changed when I got to college.

Like I said, I wanted to start a new life and be someone new, definitely not the love-struck teenager I was. I was determined to make the best out of everything and keep moving forward. I never thought twice about that flier again, until my friend randomly asked me to go with her to see if it was something she wanted to do since she was scared to go alone.

Long story short, my friend ended up bailing and I was stuck going on a fall retreat with a bunch of college students I had never met. I tried to get myself out of going several times using my best excuses. I reluctantly borrowed a sleeping bag and went. A weekend away with complete strangers sounded a bit too familiar to me. When we arrived at the retreat, it was clear everyone already knew each other or at least each other's names. But even though I didn't know anyone, I didn't feel alone, and that felt odd to me. I am used to being all alone, so whenever that feeling changes, I get unsettled. I tried my best to make friends around me, but everyone seemed to have already settled into their friend groups. I didn't mind sitting on the outside of things, I liked to see how differently they all interacted. Boys were blue, girls were pink, and no purple was allowed. We had great speakers and worship leaders that truly captured the sense of community. As strange as these people were, I liked that they were different.

I have always said that that Jesus captured my heart at that fall retreat. I loved everything about Him, everything he stood for love, peace, and forgiveness. But the thing that made me interested in following him the most, was His claim to be God. In Islam, to claim anyone is equal to Allah is an unforgivable sin and to claim that Jesus is the Son of God guarantees the loss of their salvation. The deity of Jesus is what differentiates Christianity from all other religions or "truths" in the world. All I ever cared about was finding the truth, and the truth that I found was that in Jesus, and Jesus alone, can salvation be found

CHAPTER SIX: THE PURSUIT OF HAPPINESS

and eternity be guaranteed. Jesus has always been and always will be the only God to show love first. He was the only God who came to me calling me His daughter. So why wouldn't I want to believe in that? Why wouldn't I want to believe that there's a God out there that sees me, loves me and would die for me? Why wouldn't I want to worship this God? Of all the gods out there, who is greater? Kinder? More loving?

And even though I did not understand this at the time, and it seemed too good to be true, everything in me wanted to believe anyway, so I did. Anyone who knew me back then would have laughed at the idea of me ever wanting to give up the "thirsty Thursday life," so only imagine the comments and questions I got when people found out that I had given it all up for a Bible study. Honestly, I thought I was just going through a phase. You know, the "I'm now going to try and get my life together" phase. Little did I know that the way I was trying to get my life together, turned out to be the cause of it falling apart.

Soon after I became a Christian, I lost most of my friends, my grades suffered, and I was labeled as the "boring Jesus freak". I remember sitting in my dorm room crying because it was the first time that I had actually been physically alone since I started college. It's easy to surround yourself with distractions: friends, drugs, boys, etc. And for the first time in my adult life, I didn't have any of it. But as I sat there, it dawned on me; I didn't feel alone. I felt scared, angry, hurt, rejected, misunderstood, but I never felt alone.

Since becoming a Christian, I have wrestled with drug abuse, physical abuse, feeling rejected and shamed, all of which have led to a violent battle with an eating disorder. No one ever said being a Christian was going to be easy. In fact, every time Jesus would call people to follow him, time and time again, we'd hear him say how difficult it would be. He repeatedly said that to follow him meant death to ourselves. I don't know if you've ever tried death, but in case you didn't know, it hurts. Parts of you, parts that you actually, really loved at one point, die. They die for the sake of a new part to be born, a new creation, a creation that is constantly being transformed into a better and fuller image of the One who has rescued you. But like I said, hard.

I think people forget that. I think they forget the weight that surrendering everything to follow Jesus carries. Being a real Christian takes everything. It can't just be a part of your life;

CHAPTER SIX: THE PURSUIT OF HAPPINESS

it is your life. During His ministry on earth, Jesus asked his followers to give their life to Him, and they were offended. They were willing to give Jesus a part of them. But to ask for the whole thing? That was just outrageous. Their exact response was, "Who can listen to it?" This call to surrender everything offended people so much that even most of the people who claimed to adore Jesus, left. "So Jesus said to the twelve, 'Do you want to go away as well?' Simon Peter answered him, 'Lord, to whom shall we go? You have the words of eternal life, and we have believed, and have to come to know, that you are the Holy One of God.'" (John 6:67-69)

As I sat in my college room, I questioned the decision I'd made thinking, "This is too hard; do I wish to just walk away as well?" As soon as I asked that question, I thought about how great my old life was, and I knew my answer. Walk away to where? Where else could I go? What other option really was there?

I thought about everything my old life and this world had to offer me. All the empty promises of comfort, happiness, love and security. I could go back to those things. I really could just choose to turn away from it all and simply go back to being the "life of the party" and chasing after every desire. I would be completely free to do and be whomever I wanted to be. I would be free but alone. And that was a feeling I never wanted to feel again.

CHAPTER SEVEN:
THE PERFECT TRAGEDY

Easy, Breezy, Beautiful Cover Girl. This is the person I spent most of my life trying to be. Beautifully light and breezy. All I ever wanted was to be seen and known as a funny, easy-going, happy person. I wanted to be known as the life of the party, not the person who killed it. Let's be honest, who really wants to hang out with a sad and frankly depressing person?

Literally no one.

But what do you do when you actually are that depressing person? What do you do when most of your life was sad and all those "get to know you" games turn out to be not so easy and breezy anymore? I will tell you one thing, it's draining. Having to continuously forge the tragedies of my life into comedies for the sake of others' comfort is frankly too exhausting. There will never be enough money or Xanax or rose-infused eye cream in the world to numb away the pain of isolation, fear, and perfectionism that haunted me.

And I have always been my own worst enemy, allowing so many wrongdoings and hurtful judgments by others to define my identity and self-worth. In fear of facing rejection, I lived my life just plainly, assuming I wasn't worth getting to know. I reasoned that since I couldn't fully accept who I was, how could I expect anyone else to? So instead of giving people the genuine opportunity to get to know me, I became a chameleon, a person of camouflage, a person who always wore an ever-changing mask.

But how was I or anyone else going to know and love someone who doesn't exist? Though it was easier for me to become the person people wanted me to be, I never gave people a fair chance to see and know who I really was. But for others to see the real me would take far more courage and vulnerability than I was willing to risk. In a world where perfectionism seems to reign, the simple acknowledgment of needing to be seen and connected only leaves us feeling more naked and afraid. We are all so terrified of being seen for who we truly are, that we've built a billion-dollar industry to protect us from ever facing that kind of vulnerability.

All my life I've been too ashamed of sharing my past, and

CHAPTER SEVEN: THE PERFECT TRAGEDY

even though it surely doesn't define me, it's certainly a part of me. It's the part that I've spent years trying to bury, always hating and shaming it for the prison I thought it kept me in. But little did I know, it would turn out to be the only part of me that could actually set me free.

Through everything, I have learned that life can still be good despite being hard. Why? Because God is good. Good, all the time. His peace is with us forever. Instead of continually searching for that next thing that will make you happy, I hope you open the eyes of your heart to see Who's been standing by your side this whole time. Jesus stands day after day, knocking on your heart to welcome Him. But to truly follow Jesus requires us to surrender everything, including who we thought we were or thought we wanted to be. Jesus didn't come and die just to be a "part" of who we are; He IS who we are.

From the outside looking in, people now would look at me and think that I've had a dream life. With one simple look, people would see a vibrant young woman "who has everything"- an amazing husband, wonderful daughter, loving parents and siblings, and a meaningful career. And to some people, my life may look like a picture-perfect image on Instagram, but that one "perfect" image that everyone wants to see, will never be able to tell my whole story. Only I can do that.

We can lie to everyone, including ourselves, but pictures are worth a thousand words for a reason. Pictures are meant to represent the truth, not dictate it. And despite our best efforts to create that flawless picture, it will always reveal the unseen brokenness we try so hard to hide. But it is only with Jesus' help, that we are able to surrender our brokenness, and finally allow ourselves to be fully seen and loved.

Milton Keynes UK
Ingram Content Group UK Ltd.
UKHW020745080124
435661UK00017B/955